P9-AGT-096

SUMMARY

of

Grit

The Power of Passion and

Perseverance

by Angela Duckworth

COMPANIONREADS

Dear readers:

This is an unofficial summary & analysis of Angela Duckworth's *Grit* designed to enrich your reading experience. Buy the original book here:

https://bit.ly/duckworthsgrit

Disclaimer: All Rights Reserved. No part of this publication may be reproduced or retransmitted, electronic or mechanical, without the written permission of the publisher; with the exception of brief quotes used in connection in reviews written for inclusion in a magazine or newspaper.

This eBook is licensed for your personal enjoyment only. This eBook may not be resold or given away to other people. If you would like to share this book with another person, please purchase an additional copy for each recipient. If you're reading this book and did not purchase it, or it was not purchased for your use only, then please purchase your own copy.

Product names, logos, brands, and other trademarks featured or referred to within this publication are the property of their respective trademark holders. These trademark holders are not affiliated with us and they do not sponsor or endorse our publications. This book is unofficial and unauthorized. It is not authorized, approved, licensed, or endorsed by the aforementioned interests or any of their licensees.

The information in this book has been provided for educational and entertainment purposes only.

The information contained in this book has been compiled from sources deemed reliable and it is accurate to the best of the Author's knowledge; however, the Author cannot guarantee its accuracy and validity and cannot be held liable for any errors or omissions. Upon using the information contained in this book, you agree to hold harmless the author from and against any damages, costs, and expenses, including any legal fees, potentially resulting from the application of any of the information provided by this guide. The disclaimer applies to any damages or injury caused by the use and application, whether directly or indirectly, of any advice or information presented, whether for breach of contract, tort, neglect, personal injury, criminal intent, or under any other cause of action. You agree to accept all risks of using the information presented inside this book.

The fact that an individual or organization is referred to in this document as a citation or source of information does not imply that the author or publisher endorses the information that the individual or organization provided. This is an unofficial summary and analytical review and has not been approved by the original author of the book.

Attention: My <u>FREE</u> Gift To You

As A Way to Say "Thank You" for being a fan of our series, I've Included a Free Gift For You:

Get How To Learn More Effectively...

For You, Free.

If you'd like one, please visit:

http://www.companionreads.com/gift

The CompanionReads Team

TABLE OF CONTENTS

BOOK ABSTRACT AND ABOUT THE AUTHOR

Main Idea:

Have you ever wondered why some people never give up, no matter what obstacles come their way? The answer is, in a word, grit. The teacher that works late into the night researching new teaching methods to reach her most difficult students. The doctor who trains hour upon hour perfecting a new surgical technique that others have given up on. The athlete who throws hundreds of passes over and over until he gets it right. Despite the differences in their professions, one thing links them together: the passion and perseverance that they have for their calling.

It may be easy to think that these people are just special and that most people will be stuck in mediocrity, but the truth is that people can increase their amount of grit. In this book, MacArthur Fellowship recipient and psychologist Dr. Angela Duckworth shares both her own and others' research regarding how grit can lead to success. She also gives a plan for people to follow to increase their amount of grit. By weaving stories of her own life with scientific studies, MacArthur creates a readable, inspiring book that readers will reference again and again.

CHAPTER BY CHAPTER ANALYSIS

Preface

Main Idea:

Although Duckworth's father repeatedly bemoaned her lack of genius-level IQ, Duckworth went on to win a prestigious award honoring her work studying the qualities that lead to success.

Supporting Ideas:

When she was growing up, Duckworth's father frequently worried aloud that his children's lack of genius would hamper their abilities to be successful in the future. Duckworth wishes that she could go back in time to reassure her father that although she may not be the smartest person, she will strive to be the grittiest and never give up.

Key Thoughts:

"A girl that is told repeatedly that she's no genius ends up winning an award for being one. The award goes to her because she has discovered that what we eventually accomplish may depend more on our passion and perseverance than on our innate talent."

PART 1: WHAT GRIT IS AND WHY IT MATTERS

Chapter 1: Showing Up

Main Idea:

Although talent and luck play a part in success, when it comes to facing a wide variety of challenges, the most successful people display a large amount of grit.

Supporting Ideas:

When Duckworth studied dropout rates among cadets at West Point, she learned that even though the cadets were all intelligent, physically fit, and overall impressive, the ones who survived Beast scored highest on the Grit Scale.

She also used the Grit Scale to successfully predict who would leave sales jobs, graduate from high school, pursue higher learning, and complete the Selection Course for the Green Berets.

She tested the Grit Scale on competitors in the Scripps National Spelling Bee and on Ivy League graduates, each time concluding that although talent is important in success, successful people also have a high amount of grit.

Key Thoughts:
"The highly accomplished were paragons of perseverance."

"In sum, no matter the domain, the highly successful had a kind of ferocious determination that played out in two ways. First, these exemplars were unusually resilient and hardworking. Second, they knew in a very, very deep way what it was they wanted. They not only had determination, they had *direction*. It was this combination of passion and perseverance that made high achievers special. In a word, they had grit."

"Our potential is one thing. What we do with it is quite another."

Chapter 2: Distracted by Talent

Main Idea:

Many times talented people are not the highest achievers; instead, people who work incredibly hard can be more successful.

Supporting Ideas:

When Duckworth first became a math teacher, she assumed that the students who showed innate mathematical talent would make the highest grades. However, she quickly began to realize that the students who worked the hardest and took the class seriously outpaced the more mathematically talented students. Interested in the relationship between hard work and success, Duckworth's experiences as a teacher lead her to become a psychologist.

Duckworth began to study psychology and learned that many others have questioned what qualities cause people to be successful.

When Francis Galton published a study on success, he posited that successful people possessed "ability", a high level of "zeal", and "the capacity for hard labor." Charles Darwin argued that zeal and hard work were the factors that lead to success, and that ability, talent, or intellect did not greatly affect a person's chance of being successful. According to Darwin's autobiography, although he was fairly intelligent, his success stemmed from a love of science and the fact that he never stopped observing the natural world. Harvard psychologist William James also argued that many people do not challenge themselves and therefore are not as successful as they could be. Chia-Jung Tsay performed experiments that proved that although the majority of people may say that hard work is more important than innate ability, people have a preference towards those with natural talent.

Before she began teaching, Duckworth worked for McKinsey, a consulting firm in New York, where talent was highly prized above all else. The partners of the firm wrote a report called "The War for Talent", in which they asserted that what makes companies successful is having the most talented people on their staff. A few journalists have pointed out that in cases of companies like Enron, having the most talented people was actually a negative because people were so intent on proving their worth to the company that they engaged in unscrupulous business practices.

Scott Kaufman, a colleague of Duckworth's, attended a school for children with learning disabilities and scored low on an IQ test. A teacher felt that he needed more challenging classes, which make him want to see what he could achieve. After excelling at the cello, he was admitted to Carnegie Melon was eventually able to switch his major from music to psychology, which was what he really wanted to study.

Duckworth feels that although tests of talent are imperfect, the real problem is that the focus on talent distracts people from focusing on effort, which is more important to success.

Key Thoughts:

"And why do we assume that it is our talent, rather than our effort, that will decide where we end up in the very long run?"

"The 'naturalness bias' is a hidden prejudice against those who've achieved what they have because they worked for it, and a hidden preference for those whom we think arrived at their place in life because they're naturally talented."

"In my view, the biggest reason a preoccupation with talent can be harmful is simple: By shining our spotlight on talent, we risk leaving everything else in the shadows. We inadvertently send the message that these other factors—including grit—don't matter as much as they really do."

Chapter 3: Effort Counts Twice

Main Idea:

In developing talent into success, effort matters twice as much as natural ability.

Supporting Ideas:

In his study "The Mundanity of Excellence", Dan Chambliss asserts that competitive swimmers excel not due to mere talent, but because of consistent training.

According to Nietzsche, the belief that talent is the reason for success gives people an excuse to avoid hard work.

Duckworth created two equations to explain how people can transition natural talent into achievement: talent x *effort*=skill and skill x *effort*=achievement.

Warren McKenzie, John Irving, and Will Smith are well-known examples of people who valued effort over their natural ability.

This effort has lead to success in their respective careers.

Harvard University researchers created a Treadmill Test that measured how much people were willing to push themselves. When psychiatrist George Vaillant followed up with the test subjects forty years later, he found that the men who had stayed on the treadmill the longest were the most successful.

Key Thoughts:

"Talent is how quickly your skills improve when you invest effort. Achievement is what happens when you take your acquired skills and use them."

"Talent—how fast we improve in skill— absolutely matters. But effort factors into the calculations *twice*, not once. Effort builds skill. At the very same time, effort makes skill *productive*."

"Even more than the effort a gritty person puts in on a single day, what matters is that they wake up the next day, and the next, ready to get on that treadmill and keep going."

"Without effort, your talent is nothing more than your unmet potential. Without effort, your skill is nothing more than what you could have done but didn't. With effort, talent becomes skill and, at the very same time, effort makes skill *productive*."

Chapter 4: How Gritty Are You?

Main Idea:

To be successful, a person should set a top-level goal and then ensure that he is working towards that goal and not wasting time on things that are distracting.

Supporting Ideas:

Jeffrey Gettleman, the East Africa bureau chief for the New York Times, set a top-level goal that he wanted to live in East Africa. To accomplish this goal, he became a journalist, starting at his college newspaper and working his way up to the New York Times, then becoming the East Africa bureau chief.

Pete Carroll, the Seattle Seahawks coach, adheres to the life philosophy *"Do things better than they have ever been done before."*

Goals can be imagined as belonging to a hierarchy, with the top-level goal on the top, mid-level goals in the center, and low-level goals at the bottom. Low- and mid-level goals should support a person's top-level goal, and any lower-level goals that do not support the top-level goal should be eliminated.

Warren Buffett has a three-step process for prioritizing career goals. First, list twenty-five career goals. Second, circle the top five most important. Third, strongly avoid the other twenty goals because they will distract you from your priorities. Duckworth would add a fourth step: decide if the goals reflect a common purpose because the more aligned your goals are, the more focused your passion will be.

New Yorker cartoonist Bob Mankoff was rejected over 2,000 times by the *New Yorker* before they accepted one of his cartoons.

Stanford psychologist Catharine Cox studied accomplished historical figures and found that although they all had similar intelligence levels, what distinguished the highest achievers was their perseverance and dedication to a single task.

Key Thoughts:

"Grit is about working on something you care about so much that you're willing to stay loyal to it."

"Grit has two components: passion and perseverance."

"What I mean by passion is not that you have something that you care about. What I mean is that you care about that *same* ultimate goal in an abiding, loyal, steady way."

Chapter Five: Grit Grows

Main Idea:

Grit may be partially genetic but it can also grow through maturity and life circumstances.

Supporting Ideas:

When the Grit Scale was administered to over 2,000 pairs of teenage twins, it showed that perseverance is 37 percent inherited and passion is 20 percent inherited. This means that genetics plays some role in a person's amount of grit but also that a person's amount of grit can increase.

Extreme changes in height and IQ scores over the past century show how a person's environment can influence their traits.

According to Duckworth's findings, many young adults have much lower grit scales than older adults do. This may be due to the culture in which the older adults were raised, but is more likely the result of maturity and experience.

There are four things that the grittiest people have in common: interest, practice, purpose, and hope.

Key Thoughts:

"...grit grows as we figure out our life philosophy, learn to dust ourselves off after rejection and disappointment, and learn to tell the difference between low-level goals that should be abandoned quickly and higher-level goals that demand more tenacity."

"One form of perseverance is the daily discipline of trying to do things better than we did yesterday."

"What ripens passion is the conviction that your work matters."

PART 2: GROWING GRIT FROM THE INSIDE OUT

Chapter 6: Interest

Main Idea:

It takes time and diligence to discover and deepen one's interest.

Supporting Ideas:

According to research, people are happier and perform better in their careers when they are doing something that they enjoy.

Many successful people who love their careers did not always have a singular passion for their work; they experimented with other things before arriving to their true passion.

According to psychologist Barry Schwartz, many young people have trouble deciding on a specific career interest because their expectations are unrealistic. They think that they will automatically love everything about their career and do not take into account that interests can deepen over time.

Interests cannot be developed in a vacuum; young people need a support network to encourage their interests.

The grittiest people don't just discover their interest, they deepen it as well.

Key Thoughts:
"Nobody is interested in everything, and everyone is interested in something. So matching your job to what captures your attention and imagination is a good idea. It may not guarantee happiness and success, but it sure helps the odds."

"...passion for your work is a little bit of *discovery*, followed by a lot of *development*, and then a lifetime of *deepening*."

"For the beginner, novelty is anything that hasn't been encountered before. *For the expert, novelty is nuance.*"

Chapter 7: Practice

Main Idea:

The most successful people not only practice longer than others, but they also deliberately practice on improving their weaknesses.

Supporting Ideas:

Deliberate practice begins by setting a stretch goal, which refers to a particular weakness that the person is trying to improve. Once the person sets the goal, he focuses solely on improving that weakness by practicing and getting feedback from others on how he can improve. Then the person practices continuously until he can easily do the thing that he once found difficult. Once he has mastered the stretch goal, he sets another. Mastering many small goals leads to great success.

Deliberate practice does not work only for athletes; many other professionals, such as writers, business people, and doctors, can benefit from deliberate practice.

When Duckworth and cognitive psychologist Anders Ericsson studied precisely how the grittiest children succeeded at the National Spelling Bee, they found that the children who had practiced deliberately advanced to further rounds far more than those who used another type of practice.

Although deliberate practice leads to success, it is incredibly difficult and exhausting.

Psychologist Mihaly Csikszentmihalyi feels that the true mark of an expert isn't deliberate practice, but flow. Flow occurs when an expert is completing a difficult task but feels like it is effortless.

Duckworth feels that deliberate practice can lead to increased states of flow. In other words, the more a person prepares, the more he can enjoy and relax during a performance.

Grittier people enjoy the hard work involved in deliberate practice more than less gritty people do.

To get the most out of deliberate practice, a person should understand why he needs to practice deliberately, make deliberate practice a habit, and change his attitude toward deliberate practice.

Key Thoughts:

"Rather than focus on what they already do well, experts strive to improve specific weaknesses. They intentionally seek out challenges they can't yet meet."

"What follows mastery of a stretch goal? Then experts start all over again with a *new* stretch goal. One by one, these subtle refinements add up to dazzling mastery."

"Flow is performing at high levels of challenge and yet feeling 'effortless,' like 'you don't have to think about it, you're just doing it.'"

"*...Gritty people do more deliberate practice* and *experience more flow.*"

Chapter 8: Purpose

Main Idea:

Purpose is the desire and aim to help others.

Supporting Ideas:

The passion of a gritty person is comprised of both interest and purpose.

Most people begin with a self-oriented interest, hone that interest through practice, and finally find a way to bring purpose into their work.

All people are designed to chase pleasure and purpose, but grittier people are vastly more motivated than others to chase purpose to a much higher degree than other people are.

Workers can be divided into three categories: those that consider their work a job, or a necessity; those that consider their work a career, or an opportunity to advance to a more prestigious position; and those who consider their work a calling, or one of the most meaningful parts of their life.

A job can slowly evolve into a calling if the worker actively looks for ways that his work can make the world a better place.

Workers who are both self-and other-motivated have the greatest success, meaning that a worker must have both a passion and a purpose for their work in order to be the most successful.

According to developmental psychologist Bill Damon, to become more purposeful, a worker should identify his interest, find a purposeful role model, discover a problem that needs solving, and then realize that he can be part of solving the problem.

To begin developing a sense of purpose, Duckworth shares three recommendations borrowed from the purpose experts she has quoted in this chapter. David Yeager suggests thinking about how the work a person is already doing can benefit society. Amy Wrzesniewski recommends that workers brainstorm small ways that they can adapt their work to fit their values. Bill Damon advises people to find a purposeful role model.

Key Thoughts:

"At its core, the idea of purpose is the idea that what we do matters to people other than ourselves."

"How you *see* your work is more important than your job title. And this means that you can go from job to career to calling—all without changing your occupation."

"Whatever your age, it's never too early or late to begin cultivating a sense of purpose."

Chapter 9: Hope

Main Idea:

Gritty people embrace an optimistic growth mindset that helps them overcome setbacks.

Supporting Ideas:

Rather than passively waiting for things to get better, people with grit believe that they can develop a better future for themselves.

In 1964, Marty Seligman and Steve Maier conducted an experiment where they showed that suffering does not lead to hopelessness; instead it is a person's perceived lack of control over his own suffering that causes him to feel hopeless. At the time, conventional wisdom said that people and animals simply react to both the good and painful things that happen to them. However, this experiment and many others showed that thoughts influence behavior, so people can have learned helplessness or learned optimism.

Both optimists and pessimists experience troubles, but optimists assume that the cause of their trouble is not permanent and can be fixed, while pessimists believe that their suffering will never end and allow their feelings about hard times to influence other parts of their lives. The grittiest people do not focus on their disappointments; they simply use them as learning tools.

Psychiatrist Aaron Beck was the first to suggest that all mental illnesses did not have their root in childhood trauma. Instead, the same event, such as losing a job, can lead to different reactions in different people. The person who reacts pessimistically may tell himself that he will never get another job, while the more optimistic person may be disappointed to lose the job but will parlay the skills he learned in that job into his next endeavor. In cognitive behavior therapy, patients can examine their self-talk and learn to change it from pessimistic to optimistic.

People who hold a fixed-mindset view believe that a person cannot change his basic intelligence level even though he can learn new skills. People who hold a growth-mindset view believe that it is possible for people to get smarter if they have opportunities, try, and believe they can. A fixed mindset can hinder people because if they encounter an obstacle, they will believe that they cannot overcome it, whereas a person with a growth mindset is operating from a core belief that intelligence is not static and therefore he can overcome obstacles with the right training. People with a growth mindset are much grittier than people with a fixed mindset.

People develop mindsets in childhood by observing how authority figures react to success and failure. For example, if a teacher or parent gets aggravated or embarrassed by a child's mistakes, the child will believe that making mistakes is bad and will not want to try. If a parent or teacher praises a child's natural ability instead of his effort, the child will believe that he cannot succeed at anything that is difficult and that he should only stick with things that come easily to him. However, if a parent or teacher shows himself making mistakes and learning from them and praises a child's effort while encouraging the child to improve, the child will have a better chance of developing a growth mindset and believing that he can succeed.

According to Duckworth, people can teach themselves hope by believing that talent and intelligence are not static, practicing positive self-talk, and asking for someone to encourage them.

Key Thoughts:

"The hope that gritty people have has nothing to do with luck and everything to do with getting up again."

"When you keep searching for ways to change your situation for the better, you stand a chance of finding them. When you stop searching, assuming they can't be found, you guarantee they won't."

"Ultimately, adopting a gritty perspective involves recognizing that people get better at things—they *grow*. Just as we want to cultivate the ability to get up off the floor when life has knocked us down, we want to give those around us the benefit of the doubt when something they've tried isn't a raging success."

"A fixed mindset about ability leads to pessimistic explanations of adversity, and that, in turn, leads to both giving up on challenges and avoiding them in the first place. In contrast, a growth mindset leads to optimistic ways of explaining adversity, and that, in turn, leads to perseverance and seeking out new challenges that will ultimately make you even stronger."

PART 3: GROWING GRIT FROM THE OUTSIDE IN

Chapter 10: Parenting for Grit

Main Idea:

Wise parents who are equal parts supportive and demanding and who model grit in their own lives are far more likely to have gritty children.

Supporting Ideas:

Some people believe that children become gritty by being raised by authoritarian parents who withhold affection. Others believe that children develop grit when given total affection and support. Duckworth interviewed Steve Young and Francesca Martinez, two successful people raised by parents with seemingly opposite parenting styles, to see which parenting approach produced children with more grit.

When Steve Young was a child, his parents would not let him quit any activities, even those he was not originally good at. As a young adult, any time he encountered adversity and wanted to quit, his dad would not let him. Although Young's parents were strict, they were also very supportive and cognizant of his emotional needs, nurturing him through severe separation anxiety when he was a child. Young feels that his parents' tough love was underscored by selflessness and his parents' desire for him to succeed.

Francesca Martinez's parents fully supported her decision to drop out of high school to pursue a career as a comic. They felt that their children should be able to follow their passions and that they should trust their children's decisions. However, when Martinez was a child, her parents made her complete demanding physical therapy exercises to combat her cerebral palsy even though she did not want to. They also did not allow television in their house.

Both families were supportive and strict in their own ways, and both families produced successful, gritty children.

Most psychologists recognize four parenting types: authoritative, which Duckworth refers to as "wise"; authoritarian; neglectful; and permissive. Wise parenting involves being equal parts demanding and supportive. Authoritarian parents are demanding but not supportive, neglectful parents are neither demanding nor supportive, and permissive parents are supportive but not demanding. Children of people who practice wise parenting are happier, more successful, and grittier than any of their counterparts.

Children instinctively mimic adults, but as children grow they are able to question other's actions. When parents are wise and gritty, their children want to be like them. Teachers and other authority figures can also play a wise parenting role in children's lives.

Key Thoughts:

"Growing up with support, respect, and high standards confers a lot of benefits, one of which is especially relevant to grit—in other words, wise parenting encourages children to *emulate* their parents."

"If you want to bring forth grit in your child, first ask how much passion and perseverance you have for your own life goals. Then ask yourself how likely it is that your approach to parenting encourages your child to emulate you. If the answer to the first question is 'a great deal,' and your answer to the second is 'very likely,' you're already parenting for grit."

"Not every grit paragon has had the benefit of a wise father and mother, but every one I've interviewed could point to *someone* in their life who, at the right time and in the right way, encouraged them to aim high and provided badly needed confidence and support."

Chapter 11: The Playing Fields of Grit

Main Idea:

Students who participate in an extracurricular activity for at least two years are more successful later in life because extracurricular activities teach discipline and persistence.

Supporting Ideas:

Psychologist Margo Gardner found that students who took part in the same extracurricular activity for two years were more likely to be employed and to make more money as adults than those who did not.

In 1978, Warren Willingham directed the Personal Qualities Project, which was designed to determine what personal characteristics caused people to be successful. The project tested over one hundred characteristics and followed a group of students from their senior year in high school to five years later. Willingham considered three areas of success: academics, leadership, and accomplishment. Follow-through was the quality that predicted the greatest success in adulthood, and students who had been in two extracurricular activities for at least two years each and had distinguished themselves in these activities had the highest follow-through rating by far. The students with the highest follow-through ratings were more likely to graduate college with honors, hold leadership positions, and make noteworthy accomplishments in a variety of areas.

Inspired by the Personal Qualities Project, Duckworth sought to replicate its results. She met with Bill and Melinda Gates, who were also interested in whether extracurricular activities are a predictor for later academic success. She scored 1,200 students using the Grit Grid in which students earned points by participating in extracurricular activities and found that the higher a student's grit score, the more likely the student was to stay in college.

Following through on commitments to extracurricular activities may produce grit, but it also requires grit. Students who are economically disadvantaged rarely get a chance to participate in extracurricular activities and, as a result, do not have a chance to develop as much grit as other students.

Psychologist Robert Eisenberger has done many experiments testing whether doing something difficult teaches a person to do other things that are difficult. His conclusion is that not only can the connection between hard work and reward be learned, but also people and animals who do not learn this connection will become lazy.

Duckworth's family follows the Hard Thing Rule, which is comprised of three parts: everyone must do a hard thing, no one can quit until he fulfills his commitment, and each person gets to pick his own hard thing. While growing grit, this also helps Duckworth's children have some independence.

Key Thoughts:

"There are countless research studies showing that kids who are more involved in extracurriculars fare better on just about every conceivable metric—they earn better grades, have higher self-esteem, are less likely to get in trouble and so forth."

"With practice, industriousness can be learned."

Chapter 12: A Culture of Grit

Main Idea:

Culture has the ability to shape our identity, so if we are part of a gritty culture, we can become grittier people.

Supporting Ideas:

A culture is comprised of a group of people who have the same values. There are sports teams, businesses, and schools that qualify as a culture. After a while of belonging to a certain culture, people will begin to assimilate that culture's values into their own identities. Gritty people will sometimes live their lives in ways that are confusing to others because the rewards for what they are doing are so far off, but their culture and identity can explain why they make hard choices.

The Finnish word *sisu* can be translated to mean perseverance or inner strength. Two lessons we can learn from the concept of *sisu* are that if we believe we can overcome adversity we probably will and that when things seem impossible, we just need to keep going.

Leaders from vastly different industries can all develop a culture of grit by having and following core values. Many people in gritty cultures discuss core values often so that the values become engrained in their identities.

Key Thoughts:

"Whether we realize it or not, the culture in which we live, and with which we identify, powerfully shapes just about every aspect of our being."

"The bottom line on culture and grit is: *If you want to be grittier, find a gritty culture and join it. If you're a leader, and you want the people in your organization to be grittier, create a gritty culture.*"

Chapter 13: Conclusion

Main Idea:

Growing grit in your life will help you achieve long-term goals and overall be happier and more successful.

Supporting Ideas:

People can grow grit in two ways: from the inside out by finding an interest, practicing, having a purpose, and hoping, and from the outside in by belonging to a culture of gritty people.

A person's levels of grit and happiness positively correlate, meaning that grittier people are happier.

Duckworth feels that although grit is important, it is not possible to say that it is the most vital personality trait because there are so many other personality traits that are important.

Encouraging excellence in children has much less to do with turning them into amazing athletes or artists and much more to do with helping them develop their grit.

Key Thoughts:
" We all face limits—not just in talent, but in opportunity. But more often than we think, our limits are self-imposed."

"To be gritty is to keep putting one foot in front of the other. To be gritty is to hold fast to an interesting and purposeful goal. To be gritty is to invest, day after week after year, in challenging practice. To be gritty is to fall down seven times, and rise eight."

THANK YOU

Hope you've enjoyed your reading experience!

We here at CompanionReads will always strive to deliver to you the highest quality guides.

So, we'd like to thank you for supporting us and reading until the very end.

Before you go, would you mind leaving us a review on Amazon?

It means a lot to us and supports us in creating high quality guides for you in the future.

Thanks once again and here's where you can leave us a review:

http://bit.ly/1clickreview

Warmly yours,

The CompanionReads Team

77696600R00035

Made in the USA
San Bernardino, CA
26 May 2018